Published by O'Connor Publishing

ISBN: 979-8-234-05908-6

To Mary Lou

From the moment we met, everything we have done, and continue to do, has been shaped by our regard for one another. Our shared love is essential to my life story. God has blessed us with a beautiful family, and through your compassion and understanding, we remain close not only as family, but also as friends. Your presence brings purpose to my life.

Contents

Preface

I began writing this book several years before I retired, almost on a whim. Looking back, I think it was my way of preparing for the inevitable: first, by recounting the experiences and lessons from my career, and second, by attempting to carve out a direction forward for a seamless and optimistic pathway into retirement.

As I gained momentum, I started to think that maybe my reflections could be useful to others; and perhaps even serve as a guide for those approaching retirement and wondering what comes next.

When I shared some of my early writing with friends and family, several encouraged me to think of this book not only as advice, but as a legacy, something for my children and grandchildren to hold onto. I took that as a profound compliment. I have never seen my life story as something that would qualify as a legacy. To me, it is simply the result of doing what my Dad always advised: keep your head down and do your best.

So, with deep love and respect for my Mom and Dad, I continue this project not just as my story, but as a continuation of theirs. They were the ones who planted the seeds, who gave me the tools, and who shaped the values that have carried me through. It is my wish that my experiences bring a smile to the faces of those who love me and, in some way, help them as they encounter some of the challenges of life.

I also hope that these reflections offer something meaningful to others who are preparing for or navigating retirement. You have earned this time in your life.

Make it count.

Chapter I

The Road to Retirement

I remember it like it was yesterday; and what a day it was!

It was graduation day at Fairfield University. I had my whole life ahead of me yet I celebrated as if there were no tomorrow. Our graduation was celebrated with one epic party spread across two beach cottages, aptly named The Castaways and The Crustacean.

In the whirlwind of final exams, packing up, and saying goodbye to my college mates, few of us had any concrete plans. We were stepping away from the comfort of college, a place where mistakes were part of the learning process, and into a world where mistakes had consequences. I had already been married for six months to my high school sweetheart and the love of my life, Mary Lou. In two weeks, I would begin a career that would take me to destinations yet unknown. As a marketing major, I had no specific industry in mind, but I found myself in the leather goods business where I would remain for the rest of my career.

Raised with a strong work ethic, I threw myself into that first job. Every new assignment, no matter how small, became an opportunity to learn. I worked long hours, absorbing everything I could and taking pride in doing things the right way. In time, that dedication paid off. I earned promotions, grew in responsibility, and by age thirty-five was a divisional vice president, later becoming the company's youngest corporate vice president at thirty-seven years old. With a loving wife, four wonderful children, a house, a dog, and a rewarding career, I was living the American dream. But as life so often reminds us, the road ahead is rarely straight.

A change in management brought shifting priorities and new personalities, and before long, I found myself caught in a reorganization that left me without a job.

"One of the toughest things that can happen to a man, happened to me today," I told Mary Lou when I got home that day. " I lost my job."

"Oh honey, I'm so sorry," she responded with love in her eyes.

Not once did she think of herself or the financial strain this would put on our household. Her first instinct was to offer comfort and then she went on to offer faith that things would work out.

And, as usual, she was right. Although there was quite a bit of anxiety and some sleepless nights, I was able to find another job within two weeks. It was simply another bend in the road. The real challenge was that the job was 120 miles away. We decided not to move so I commuted to work on Monday mornings and came home on Friday afternoons. It wasn't easy, but thanks to Mary Lou's strength and grace, we managed to keep our family life steady and filled with love. Our weekends were crazy busy with the usual sporting events and family activities, and I gladly participated in coaching soccer and baseball.

This was the first time in my life that I was living entirely on my own. Because it was not my real home, I intentionally planned a bare-bones existence, almost like living in a barracks. During the week, I stayed in a one-bedroom apartment. I had basic cable with three channels, slept on a cot, and survived on soup and boiled chicken. For reasons I still cannot explain, I challenged myself to make it through the first winter without using heat. My lowest point came when I was snowed in for two days with no heat, no food, and the only thing on TV was the news showing dads home from work, happily playing in the snow with their kids because all businesses were closed!

When our two oldest children, Katie and Bryan, had graduated from college and our twins, Colleen and Erin, were finishing high school, I again found myself out of work. I was learning the hard way that losing a job was a difficult part of life, but I never felt ashamed. I have always tried to conduct myself with integrity, and I have learned to trust that when one door closes, another opens and that things aways happen for a reason. I remained positive, set new goals, and kept moving forward.

This time, the new opportunity took us in an entirely different direction. Mary Lou and I bought a seaside restaurant out of bankruptcy and became restaurateurs. Our entire family joined in, even my Dad. Around the same time, my son and I started a house-painting business. A friend once told me, "find the busiest person in the room and give them more to do." I guess I took that to heart, because I also became a college rugby coach and even earned my real estate license.

Our restaurant, Tommy O'Connor's Off the Wall, was a charming spot on the Long Island Sound with beautiful water views, fine dining, and a loyal clientele. Summers were bustling; winters not so much. But the experience of working together as a family was invaluable.

There were moments of joy and laughter, and a few of frustration. The kids and I once tried to surprise Mary Lou by decorating the Christmas tree while she was at the restaurant only to have the needles fall off before she got home. (Charlie Brown's tree looked better than ours that year!) Then came Hurricane Katrina, which flooded our basement and destroyed our supplies. And there was the time we went on vacation and left Katie in charge; a story she'll have to tell herself!

Still, the good times far outweighed the bad. We made wonderful memories with friends and neighbors, celebrated countless holidays, and hosted family gatherings that will forever warm my heart. The brightest moment of all was my Dad's surprise eightieth birthday party; the look on his face and the joy in his eyes that night made every struggle worthwhile.

After a few years, we decided to sell the restaurant, close the painting business, and return to the corporate world. Not long after, I received a call from my former employer, the same company 120 miles from home. Because I had left on good terms and never burned bridges, they welcomed me back with open arms.

It was back to living alone in my spartan-like existence. It was pretty much the same routine except, this time, I allowed myself to turn on the heat and I slept on an air mattress which was quite comfortable until it got a puncture!

The road smoothed out for a while until the company was sold. A buyout brought a culture change, and although I did my best to adapt, it just wasn't the same. Still, I continued to learn, to contribute, and to focus on the positives.

After forty-three years in my career, I was approaching sixty-six and eligible for Social Security. One day, my boss called to discuss potential layoffs. When he mentioned a single mother on our team, I asked him to lay me off instead. And just like that, I retired and my family threw me a retirement party!

Not so fast.

One month later, I received an offer from my alma mater, Fairfield University, to serve as the school's first Director of Rugby. It was the ideal bridge into retirement; promoting a sport I loved, working with young men and women, and giving back to the place where my own journey began.

After fulfilling my contract and laying a strong foundation for both the men's and women's programs, I knew it was time to step aside and let someone else take the program to the next level.

At sixty-nine, I retired once again; this time for real. My granddaughter, Kaleigh, summed it up best when she said, "Pop Pop, if you go back to work again, we're not having another retirement party for you!" She was right. It was finally time.

I have come to realize that there is no ideal moment to retire, but there is always the right moment to embrace life's next chapter. After a long and fulfilling career, I am grateful to have the health, energy, and faith to enjoy the years ahead.

PRAESES ET CURATORES

Universitatis Fairfieldensis

OMNIBUS HAS LITTERAS PERLECTURIS SALUTEM IN DOMINO

THOMAS BRYAN O'CONNOR

PRO MERITIS EIUS ADMISIMUS AD GRADUM

BACCALAUREATUS SCIENTIARUM

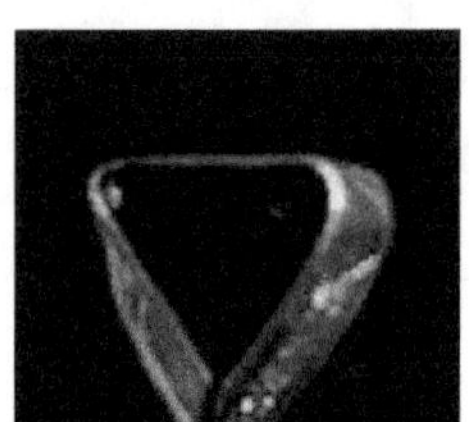

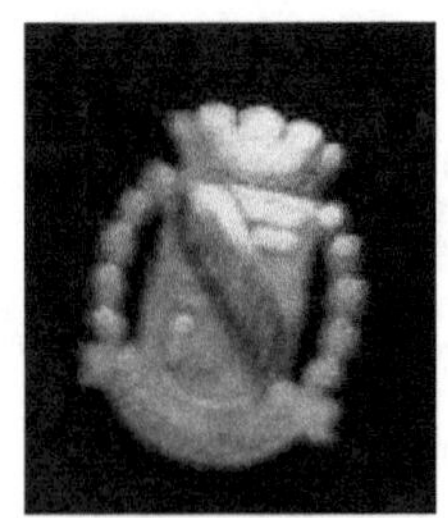

Chapter II

Don't Forget God

I believe that God is central to our lives. Taking time to pay tribute to the Supreme Being is a natural part of my life. I am incredibly fortunate to have my family, friends, and the abundance of gifts that God has provided. He plays such a powerful role in my everyday life and so it makes sense that setting aside time to pray, meditate, and reflect becomes a regular practice.

In retirement, I have been blessed with more time; time that can be devoted to deepening my relationship with God. This devotion does not necessarily mean attending church every day although I do make it a priority. I have found that going to morning Mass is a wonderful way to start my day. It is both soothing and inspirational, setting a calm and grateful tone for everything that follows.

There are countless ways to give thanks to God and one of the most meaningful is through service. I believe that volunteer work is a powerful way for retirees to express our faith. After all, God calls us to love our neighbors and what better way to do that than by helping the sick, the homeless, or the homebound. Serving others can bring a renewed sense of purpose to our lives while also enriching the lives of those we help.

Opportunities to serve are often closer than we think. Within our own parish and community, there are needs for handymen, garden or floral committees, ride sharing, religious instructors, and many others. I am a member of the Knights of Columbus providing service to others focused upon charity, unity, and fraternity.

For me, teaching religious education has been especially rewarding. Sharing lessons of faith with children and having the chance to possibly make a difference in someone's life has shaped the way I live my own. It keeps me honest and it helps me to lead by example. The time commitment is small, but the spiritual rewards are immeasurable.

God works in wonderful and often unexpected ways. While the primary motivation for helping others is not self-interest, I have found that my own involvement leads to unexpected blessings, new friendships, new opportunities, and renewed energy. Getting involved opens doors to new experiences and connections.

I have been teaching for over thirty years now. At this point, I even have students whose parents I taught when they were children! Some of them still remember my antics like standing on my head and drinking water, a gentler version of my old rugby party trick, which, admittedly, once involved beer. My students happened to be acting up a bit during one of my classes. I exclaimed, "what do I have to do to get you kids to listen to me, stand on my head?" Of course, they all cheered positively and so the rest is history. Word got around and now Mr. Tom standing on his head while drinking water is part of the program!

I enjoy making my classes fun and interactive, helping kids visualize the lessons of faith. One of my favorite examples is teaching the idea that prayer is a conversation with God. To illustrate this, I lie on the floor and pray for God to open the window. Then I get up, walk over to the window, and open it myself. I explain that God gives us the ability to act, our legs to walk, our minds to understand, and our hands to do. God answers prayers, but we must be willing participants in the process. For instance, it is not enough to just ask God to help me to pass a test; I must also study. God provides the tools, but we need to do the work.

I remember one day, as I lay on the floor delivering this lesson, the Director of Religious Education walked by.

She peeked in and said, "Mr. Tom, I've seen you stand on your head and do all kinds of things, but what exactly are you doing now?"

I smiled and replied, "Sister, I'm teaching the kids how to pray." Exasperated, she just shook her head and walked away.

My methods may be unorthodox, but I know they leave an impression. I have had former students, now adults, come up to me and tell me that they still remember our lessons from second grade Sunday school.

I believe my involvement has a positive impact not only on my students but on their families as well. It is deeply rewarding and I hope it sets a good example for others to follow. I strive to be someone others can relate to; someone whose actions inspire them to get involved themselves.

In the end, nurturing both my relationship with God and my service to others leads to an exponentially richer and more meaningful life. Retirement has given me the gift of time and I choose to spend it drawing closer to God, serving others, and living with gratitude. For me, that is what makes this season of life not just fulfilling but truly blessed.

Chapter III

Family

Other than God, no one is going to ever love me like the members of my family. Now that I am retired, I feel that I am more readily able to interact with my family and they, in turn, can appreciate me in a different way.

I do not force myself upon my family. I have spent a good portion of my time away from them because of the requirements of my career. Consequently, they are not used to me being around. If my wife announces that she's off to the mall, I don't automatically get in the car. I understand that she may be used to going to the mall by herself and that this may be her own private time. Instead, I'll say something like "when you get back let's take a walk."

Throughout my working life, I have spent most of my time juggling my career while sharing life with my wife. Retirement brings a major shift, not just for me, but for Mary Lou as well. It is important for me to remember that just because I am experiencing a big change does not mean she is on the same timeline or ready for an overhaul in daily life. So, I am trying to take it slowly. I realize that this is a transition, not a sprint. I understand that it will take time and space to adjust. I think of it as the beginning of a new chapter and maybe even a bit of a new courtship. This is a great opportunity to rediscover what first brought us together, explore fresh ways to connect, laugh, and support each other.

I realize that retirement can be an opportunity not just to relax, but to deepen a love that has already stood the test of time. Whether it is traveling, taking walks, picking up a hobby together, or simply learning how to share the TV remote again, this new phase of life is presenting a chance to grow together in a whole new way.

Some of the best parenting advice I ever received came from a dear friend who essentially told me that my children have lots of friends but only one father. So I didn't spend my time trying to be their friend but just their father. That simple but profound wisdom shaped how I raised my children. I focused on being a steady hand and a loving presence, someone my kids could always count upon.

Now that I am retired and my children are grown up with spouses and families of their own, I have found our relationships shifting in beautiful ways. I am still their father and still there to offer love, guidance, and support. But now, I also have the privilege of being their friend, someone with whom they choose to spend time, share their thoughts or even enjoy a cocktail with at the end of a long day.

I am fortunate to have not only children but also grandchildren. In this respect, retirement presents another beautiful opportunity, not simply for rest, but for deep connection. This chapter of life is filled with moments that become the very fabric of lasting memories. A round of golf, a shared ski day, sailing, beach outings, games with constantly changing rules, each becomes a chance to connect, to love, to laugh, and to share one more hug.

I once came across a sentiment about grandchildren that stayedwith me because it captured something I feel deeply. There are moments with grandchildren that seem simple like a hug, a quiet smile, a small hand resting on your cheek, a few unremarkable minutes shared by a Christmas tree. Those moments settle into a grandfather's heart and remain there permanently, becoming some of life's most lasting memories. If my grandchildren could fully understand what those brief moments mean to me, they would know how full my heart truly is.

As I get older, I begin to understand that life is not measured in milestones or material things. It is measured in the love we give and receive along the way. My grandchildren, without even realizing it, have given me some of the richest gifts of my life such as joy in ordinary moments, laughter when it was needed most, and a gentle reminder to slow down and appreciate the present.

Watching them grow has been one of my greatest privileges. Their innocence, kindness, and curiosity about the world have a way of reminding me what truly matters. In their eyes, I see hope. In their laughter, I feel a renewed sense of youth. In their affection, I feel both seen and needed in a way that is profoundly grounding.

One day they may not remember every small moment we shared, but I will. I will carry them with me always, grateful for every second I have been given. If there is one message I hope they understand someday, it is simply this: they are loved more deeply than words can ever fully express.

These are the golden years, not merely because of the leisure they afford. They are golden because of the richness of family life that surrounds them. Retirement, I have come to understand, is not just about stepping back from work, it is about leaning into what matters most.

Mary Lou and I have been especially blessed; all our children and grandchildren live in the same neighborhood. That is a rarity, and one we do not take for granted. We make the most of every opportunity to spend time together; always with respect for space and independence, never intruding, always inviting.

The strong relationships we built with our four children have naturally extended to include our grandchildren. We make it a priority to attend school activities, sporting events, and anything else that matters to them. We also carve out one-on-one time; the kind of moments that don't show up in photos but stay in your heart forever.

One tradition that brings us all together is Mary Lou's Sunday brunch after Mass. It is a simple ritual, but one filled with meaning, care, and love. I often find myself sitting back, taking in the conversations happening across the table between siblings, the playful banter amongst cousins, the occasional teasing, the constant laughter, and every now and then, a public service announcement from their patriarch! In those quiet moments of observation, I see the joy, the love, and the legacy that we have built.

We even vacation together; all sixteen of us under one roof in Stone Harbor at the Jersey shore every summer. All three generations now look forward to this annual tradition. We build sandcastles, swim in the waves, piece together community puzzles, barbecue and, perhaps my favorite tradition, gather as a family each evening to watch the sunset over the bay. Some might find that chaotic, but we find it comforting. It is a testament to the strength of our bond and the joy we find in simply being together.

I believe my deep appreciation for family stems from my Mom and Dad, along with my two brothers, Kevin & KC. Our summers at the Jersey Shore and the Adirondacks, and winters skiing in Vermont and at Gore Mountain are forever etched in my memory. One of my favorite rituals was having a catch with my Dad after dinner; a small but meaningful tradition that reminds me of that heartfelt scene in the movie Field of Dreams when Ray Kinsella famously said, "Hey Dad? Want to have a catch?" Similarly, the bond that I had with my Mom was very special. In her final days, I was incredibly humbled when she asked me to do her eulogy.

Along with our wives, my two brothers and I gather each winter in Park City for a few days of skiing, reminiscence, and tomfoolery. Kevin, the oldest, and his wife, Debbie, generously host us at their winter getaway, which has become our unofficial reunion headquarters. KC, the youngest, and his wife, Fran, fly in from Minnesota, and within minutes of arriving, conversations resume as if they had only been paused the night before.

On the slopes, old sibling roles quickly return. Kevin naturally takes the lead like a mission commander while KC and I try to prove we still possess the athleticism of our younger years, often negotiating quietly with joints that disagree. Mary Lou and Debbie have witnessed enough of the O'Connor boys' antics to wisely balance skiing with relaxation. Fran happily joins us until she discovers how much fun the other girls are having spending our money in the shops of Park City, at which point her priorities understandably shift.

What began as a simple ski trip has become a meaningful

annual tradition. These few days allow us to step away from the responsibilities that scatter us across states and return, briefly, to being three brothers bound by shared memories and laughter. As the years pass, we may ski a little slower and retire a little earlier, but the time together serves as a powerful reminder that while youth fades, the joy of family and tradition only grows stronger.

In 1992, Mom and Dad decided to host a small reunion with just Mom's boys. That weekend became the first of what is now known as The O'Connor Open (TOCO). Our spouses and children were not invited; this was just for the original five. We played golf on Saturday while Mom proudly called her friends, updating them on what time her boys would be arriving at the clubhouse for dinner. After our round, she would lead us into the clubhouse dining room like a queen with her court, her friends craning their necks to see who wore the winner's green jacket.

From those early days, TOCO has grown. We have gradually included our wives, our children, our children's spouses and, eventually, our grandchildren will be invited to play. Today, the women and men play in separate tournaments, but we all come together afterwards to celebrate as one extended family. All 29 of us!

In 2025, we celebrated the 33rd anniversary of TOCO with a special cake marking what would have been both GiGi and Pop Pop's 100th birthdays. What began as a simple family golf outing has grown into a cherished tradition, a living tribute to the love and legacy of our parents and a celebration of family. Thank you, Mom and Dad.

Chapter IV

Ditch Your Watch

For most of my life, time ran the show. I had to get to school on time, wrestling practice on time, meet work deadlines, catch the lunch bell, jump at the sound of the alarm clock and always chase the next hour or the next obligation. These days, I say ditch the watch!

Of course, there are still schedules to keep like church, medications, and family commitments. But now, I try to use my free time wisely, not let it use me. Lack of time should never be an excuse for missing my granddaughter's recital, a graduation, a chance to visit an old friend, a hospital stop or even just lingering on the beach an extra hour to watch the sunset.

After years of believing that every minute had to count, I have discovered something better; I can finally take my time. I can appreciate people and places with no rush, no pressure. My time is limited only by the span of my own life so why not stretch it out and savor it?

Mary Lou and I are blessed that all four of our children and their spouses live nearby, along with our six grandchildren. We have made it a rule in our household that if we are invited to dinner, a game, or a school play, we go. That is a priority and beyond that, we stay flexible, ready to drop what we're doing for a walk, a beach day, a round of golf, or simply coffee with a friend. I do my best not to let the clock dictate my life.

I have noticed this new mindset showing up in all sorts of small but powerful ways.

One winter morning, we were having coffee and watching the news.

I sighed, "I should have gone skiing today."

Mary Lou looked at me and said, "why don't you go?"

She was right. I wasn't used to such freedom. But I went and it felt incredible! What a terrific example of how great it is to be able to have such liberty with my time!

Not long after, the same freedom showed up in a different way. I was down at the beach doing some surf casting when the wind picked up. I thought, terrific sailing weather. Without hesitation, I packed up the fishing rod, hoisted the sails, and spent my time gliding across the water, the picture of independence, flexibility, and joy.

The same spirit carried over when I got a call from a former college classmate asking if I could be a fourth for a round of golf. In the past, I would have checked my calendar, worried about what I should be doing, or tried to squeeze it in. This time, I didn't even think twice; I said yes. Not only did I have a wonderful time, but I also met another classmate and another golfer who shared my love for skiing. We laughed, swapped stories, and made connections that never would have happened if I didn't step up to take the opportunity and just say "yes."

Not every moment has to be about adventure. Some of my favorite unplanned times are the quiet ones. Every so often, I take a walk along the beach and search for sea glass. The hunt itself is calming, but it also gives me the ideal space for deep thought and prayer. With the sound of the waves in the background and the sand under my feet, I find a kind of peace that no schedule could ever provide.

Many of my best moments come from time with my grandchildren. Every now and then, after school, I will take one or two out for ice cream. I don't make it a habit because I want it to feel special each time. On other days, I bring them home and we play games like tic-tac-toe or Connect 4. We laugh, we shout with joy, and for that stretch of time we are in our own special element. These small moments, sticky fingers from an ice cream cone or triumphant cheers over a Connect 4 win, are as meaningful as any big event.

Another favorite with the grandkids is taking them down to the beach to go garbage picking. They see it as an adventure, hunting for treasures. Before long, they realize they are also cleaning up the shore, helping the environment, and doing something good for others. What could have been a chore becomes a shared mission, full of fun and laughter. In those moments, I am not just spending time with them, I am teaching them how to use their own time with purpose. That, to me, feels like time invested, not just time passed.

Freedom from the clock does not mean wasting time, it means owning it. It means saying yes to skiing on a whim, switching from fishing to sailing because the wind invites me, grabbing my golf clubs when an old friend calls, or sharing ice cream and laughter with my grandchildren. It means teaching them that time is not just to be filled, but to be valued.

These days, my watch is the smile on a grandchild's face or the setting of the sun.

Chapter V

The Importance of Friends

My best friend happens to be my wife. After fifty years of marriage, countless shared experiences, and the incredible journey of raising a family together, that statement may not be surprising, but it is deeply meaningful. We do just about everything together, not out of habit or obligation, but because we truly enjoy each other's company. Ours is a partnership rooted in friendship and that has made all the difference.

That said, friendship extends beyond marriage. My oldest friend, Rodd, and I have shared a bond for over seventy years, a friendship that began when we were toddlers. Our parents were next-door neighbors, and they literally built a playpen between the two houses so that we could entertain each other. That simple gesture marked the start of a lifelong connection.

Rodd and I grew up side by side while playing sports, surfing, skiing, going to school, and getting into trouble (as boys do). We stood beside each other as groomsmen in each other's wedding. Our wives became fast friends and when children came along, the bond extended seamlessly to the next generation. Together, we vacationed as families while skiing in the winters and enjoying the Jersey Shore in the summers. What began as a friendship between two little boys grew into a three-generation tradition of togetherness. I doubt our parents imagined the legacy that they were nurturing, but I'm grateful every day that they did.

Friendships that endure through decades become more than just connections. They have become part of my foundation and a cherished gift I want to recognize and nurture in others. I understand the value of showing up, of listening, of being steady. It gives me quiet confidence in the importance of relationships and the wisdom to cultivate them with care.

We love our neighbors! Over thirty years ago, a small group of us were sitting on the beach one summer afternoon and chatting about the upcoming Labor Day weekend. None of us wanted to leave the island, so we began brainstorming ways to celebrate together with our families. What started as a simple idea quickly grew into a full weekend itinerary beginning with a Friday parade and ending on Labor Day Monday with a spirited adults vs. kids soccer game. In between we planned barbecues, beach games, and plenty of relaxation. I suggested that we give our gathering a name, and so CARNIVALE was born!

What began as a casual Sunday afternoon whim among six families has since blossomed into a cherished tradition, now bringing together more than 300 people under the guidance of a leader known as "the Prince of Carnivale." This multi-generational celebration not only strengthens long-standing friendships but also warmly welcomes new neighbors. Over four days, the festival showcases a one-of-a-kind community spirit that continues to thrive. Each participant receives a uniquely designed and hand-crafted necklace to commemorate the seaside event.

At the conclusion of each Carnivale, the Prince awards the "coveted Trophy of Carnivale" to the individual who best embodies the spirit of the celebration. The trophy, one that rivals the famous Stanley Cup, resides in the winner's home for one year before being returned to the Prince on the first day of the next Carnivale.

I now sit back and smile as I reminisce about the friendships that have been developed and nurtured, not only for Mary Lou & me, but for our family and neighborhood as well.

In 2004, Mary Lou and I pulled together what would become one of our most memorable adventures, a sailing trip through the British Virgin Islands. My brother took the helm as captain along with my nephew as first mate. We were joined by three other couples who are among our closest friends. Together we set off from Tortola aboard a 40-foot monohull, our floating home for the week. We explored island destinations such as Cane Garden Bay where we snorkeled in hidden coves and tied up near Virgin Gorda to explore its famous Baths. At night, we gathered on deck under a canopy of stars, swapping stories, laughing, and toasting the day's adventures. Of course, part of the fun was bar hopping by boat. We made the rounds at legendary spots like Foxy's with its infectious energy, Sidney's Peace & Love with its easy charm, and my personal favorite, the Soggy Dollar Bar. It was there that I found myself in an impromptu Ring Toss showdown with another boat crew. Somehow, I managed to win, and the prize was a round of Painkillers for our entire crew!

Even though we spent an entire week in close quarters, the laughter, the shared meals, and the teamwork of sailing brought us all even closer together. In fact, we had such a wonderful time that we ended up repeating the trip three more times. That's the kind of friendship that stands the test of time!

In 2010, Bryan and I traveled to Colorado with nine other guys for what became the ski trip of a lifetime. Over six days, we skied Breckenridge, Copper, Keystone, and Vail. We caught the first chair each morning and the last chair each afternoon. The weather was terrific, the company superb, and the laughs and stories were endless.

I took a trip to Atlantic City to meet up with Charlie, my former high school history teacher. Charlie had been in my life for decades. He was not only a teacher but also a mentor and friend. We stayed in touch over the years through calls, cards, and the occasional alumni event. We talked about getting together for some time, and we finally made it happen in Atlantic City. He was a one-armed bandit kind of guy; I was a blackjack guy. We gambled, shared some laughs, and caught up on life. It felt good to give him a little bit of attention; something he never asked for but always deserved.

In retirement, friends become even more important. They are the ones who celebrate my milestones, lift my spirits during tough times, and help turn the ordinary into something special. Whether I am venting about my golf swing, laughing over old memories, or just sharing a quiet cup of coffee, a good friend makes every moment better and offers compassion, laughter, and support.

I believe that strong friendships are also good for my health. They help to keep my mind sharp, my heart full, and my calendar pleasantly busy. Whether it's a quick phone call, a walk around the block, or a spontaneous lunch, those little connections go a long way to keep me engaged and happy. I attend a bi-monthly Zoom call with some of my college rugby mates, something we started during COVID. We keep current with one another as well as reminisce about the old beach cottages we shared while repeating old stories. The older we get, the better we were!

I had the pleasure of attending my 50th college reunion. Remarkably, after half a century, I felt even closer to my classmates than ever before. Looking back, I can only surmise that while we shared much in common during our college years, that sense of connection has grown exponentially over time. Life experiences like raising families, building careers, and navigating challenges have built an even deeper bond among us regardless of where we live or what paths we have taken. We had such a wonderful time together that many of us met to continue the reunion in Key West! Fifty years may have passed, but the friendships and the laughter have only grown stronger with time. Similarly, my high school classmates and I get together on an annual basis. Last year, we met at Monmouth Racetrack in New Jersey. Just recently, we had a golf outing and afterwards one of the guys and his wife opened their home for some food, drink, and camaraderie.

I cherish my friendships. I nurture them, show up for them, and never take them for granted. Because in the end, one of life's greatest blessings is having someone who knows all my stories and still wants to hear them again. The people in my life, those I love, those I grow with, and those who stand by me, are what gives my stories meaning.

Chapter VI

Take a Nap

Some of my most memorable naps came when my children were babies and toddlers. I'd lie back on the couch, a little one sprawled on my chest like a warm, breathing paperweight. Our breathing would sync slow, steady, and soothing until we both drifted off. There is nothing quite like waking up to find a tiny hand still resting on your chin. Now, as a grandfather, I sometimes get to relive that same joy with my grandchildren. It feels like life has given me a second chance at those cherished naps.

Bedtime was another adventure altogether. The routine was supposed to be simple: prayers, a story, and then a few lullabies. Of course, my lullabies often turned into a full-blown concert especially at Christmastime. I would belt out songs with a little too much enthusiasm. With the walls practically vibrating, Mary Lou wondered from downstairs what on earth was going on. Sometimes, the kids were wide-eyed with laughter instead of sleepy, and often, I was the one who ended up dozing off first.

It's not often that a single nap makes it into the family history books, but one in particular is unforgettable. Our twin daughters were about 18 months old when Mary Lou went shopping with our two older kids, leaving me home with a sore back and in charge of our napping babies. I stretched out on the couch downstairs and drifted into what I thought would be a harmless little nap. Upstairs, however, the twins had other plans. Instead of settling down, they decided their dresser was a jungle gym. Using the drawers as steps, they climbed up like mountaineers on an expedition until the mountain tipped over. When Mary Lou came home, she found Erin peacefully snoozing under the dresser as if it were a cozy little blanket fort, while Colleen, already cut and bruised from an earlier mishap, was fast asleep on the floor beside her. And me? Still out cold on the couch with a pulled back muscle. Quite a scene!

Naturally, the next stop was the walk-in clinic, where the doctor was required to interview each one of us separately in order to rule out foul play. Imagine the absurdity: a bruised toddler, another fresh from her dresser-top adventure, and me, the exhausted dad with a bad back, all being asked if we were mistreated. That nap definitely became legendary!

As the years went on, I learned to respect the signals my body gave me. After decades of juggling long hours, endless responsibilities, and stress that did not always quit at the end of the day, I realized that I no longer need to power through exhaustion. I have earned the right to listen to my body. Now, if I feel tired, I don't resist; I take a nap.

Some of my naps sneak up on me. I often sit down with a book in the afternoon, fully intent on reading a few chapters, only to wake up later with the book sliding off my chest and my glasses slightly askew. Other naps feel like planned indulgences, especially in the summer, when Mary Lou and I sit on the beach in the late afternoon. The waves roll in, the gulls chatter, and the sun warms everything it touches. Somewhere between conversation and silence, I drift away. That's my idea of luxury!

Science tells us that naps are good for us while lowering stress, boosting memory, and even helping the heart. But I don't need a study to convince me. I know firsthand the way a nap can reset a day, lift a mood, and remind me that rest is as essential as work.

So now, I nap without guilt. Sometimes it's twenty minutes, sometimes longer. Either way, I wake up feeling refreshed and ready to laugh at myself a little. After all, at this stage of life, I have more than earned the right to fall asleep with a book in my lap or even out snore the sound of the sea gulls!

Chapter VII

What Is Your Passion?

One of the most interesting and revealing questions I can ask someone is: "What is your passion?" It often opens the door to meaningful conversations. I once asked that question during a business trip to China. I was at dinner with two friends who were also my suppliers. The conversation had hit an awkward lull, so I asked, "What is your passion?" That single question sparked an hour-long discussion and even led to us ordering another bottle of wine. Passion connects people.

When I hear the word passion, my mind immediately turns to God. He is the source of everything I hold dear and I am grateful for all that I have been given. I try to live my life in a way that uses the grace I have received to treat others as I would like to be treated. Whether it is participating in daily Mass, interacting with my family, serving as a catechist, or helping college students with job-seeking and networking, my faith guides me. My hope is to make a difference in the life of at least one other person.

My passion for family is extreme. I find deep contentment in simply being with them, relaxing on the beach, cheering at our grandchildren's games and school events, or sharing stories over Sunday brunch. Now that I am retired, I am especially mindful of the unique gifts of my wife, my children, their spouses, and my grandchildren. I feel blessed to have fifteen family members living nearby, all of whom influence me and allow me to leave an impression on them.

One summer, my grandson Brady worked with me for a couple of hours each day. We tackled chores like power washing, painting, and yardwork. We accomplished plenty, but the best part was the conversations especially about our Irish heritage. Those talks were priceless, developing a bond that will always be ours.

I share similar relationships with each of my grandchildren. My oldest granddaughter, Kaleigh, and I can discuss anything from school to current events to our mutual love of sailing. I am impressed by her ability to multi-task amongst schoolwork, athletics, theater, and volunteering. Her maturity keeps me grounded. Her brother, William, and I share a love of surfing and silly banter. I once taught him to ski by dangling a dollar bill just out of reach to distract him from falling. I also taught him how to cut the lawn; it was great until the novelty wore off and the job returned to me!

Even the younger ones get my full attention. Jack loves helping me with recycling projects, laughing hysterically as he crushes plastic bottles and the caps fly twenty yards away. I also took him skiing for his first time at the same mountain where I taught my own children. McKenna delights in constantly beating me at tic-tac-toe, and I occasionally tuck her in at night for stories and bedtime prayers. She is the first to snuggle with me each Christmas Eve as I read The Night Before Christmas to all the kids.

And then there's Áine, the littlest. Babysitting for her brings back tender memories of my own children. She melts my heart when she whispers "Pop Pop" as I hold her close. Singing to her, as I once did to her mom, is among my favorite moments.

I love encouraging traditions that build memories with my grandkids. Every spring they help me bring my sailboat down to the beach and every fall we bring it back home. Each September, we host our own neighborhood trick-or-treat night, sending the kids door to door weeks before Halloween. Our neighbors scratch their heads, but the grandchildren cheer with delight!

Retirement has given me the chance to enjoy life more fully on my own terms. I find great joy in skiing, sailing, walking, and golf often with Mary Lou, our children and their spouses, our grandchildren, my brothers, and many friends. Some of my best conversations with my older grandchildren happen when they are a captive audience on my sailboat. These talks about what matters most often turn into the most meaningful exchanges I have ever had.

My devotion extends beyond family and is deeply rooted in the values passed down through my heritage: loyalty, generosity, and responsibility to one another. For more than fifty-five years, those values have guided my involvement in Fairfield University's rugby community where I have worn several hats: player, coach, director, and co-founder of the Friends of Fairfield Rugby.

In late 2008, a fellow alumnus brought to my attention that a freshmen rugby player was facing serious financial hardship and might not be able to return for the Spring 2009 semester without raising $5,000. It was the kind of situation my upbringing taught me not to ignore. Our long-time friend and twenty-year moderator of the Fairfield University Rugby Football Club, Paul I. Davis, urged Mary Lou and me to find a way to help. After speaking with a few trusted rugby alumni, a plan was developed that reflected the spirit of looking after our own. The founding of the PID Fund for Fairfield Rugby, a 501(c) (3) nonprofit organization was established. With the support of the rugby alumni community, enough money was raised in a short period of time to keep that young man in school. What began as an act of compassion quickly rekindled a powerful sense of shared purpose. That same spirit continues today as our organization, now known as the Friends of Fairfield Rugby, remains strong and active.

Rugby, much like the Irish culture itself, is built on tradition, camaraderie, and respect. My passion for this way of life gained friendships, cherished memories, and an enduring connection to both the men's and women's teams as they navigate their journeys at Fairfield University and beyond. In serving the rugby community, I have tried to live my values while giving back, standing alongside others, and leaving things better than I found them.

I hold our neighborhood close to my heart. For more than forty-five years, Mary Lou and I have lived in a small beach hamlet where everybody knows your name. Neighbors are kind, children play freely, and traditions bind us together. At the town green, lovingly maintained by our volunteer firefighters, Santa arrives each Christmas to hand out candy, and on Memorial Day, neighbors gather to honor those who gave their lives for our country. In the summer, Mary Lou and I host Friday night cocktails on our front porch, welcoming friends and neighbors to relax and share a laugh.

On St. Patrick's Day 2017, I was deeply honored to be named Irish Mayor for a Day by the Honorable John Harkins, then Mayor of the Town of Stratford, Connecticut. This recognition was a meaningful tribute to my lifelong passion for our Irish-American heritage. That honor became even more special when my daughter, Colleen, received the same title in 2018 with my grandson, Brady, proudly named the First Irish Leprechaun by the Honorable Laura Hoydick. In 2022, Mayor Hoydick extended that same honor to my son, Bryan. I am immensely proud that my family not only shares this passion for our heritage but actively expresses it in their own homes and community.

I am not especially handy and I have never been one to find a hobby just for the sake of it. I am content with the basics like cutting the lawn, painting, and shoveling snow so I don't feel the need to chase a pastime that does not fit me. What I have discovered is that fulfillment does not have to come from a hobby at all. It comes from faith, family, friendship, and community.

So if I am asked, "What is your passion?" my answer is simple; it isn't a thing I do, it is my trust in the Lord and His gift of the people I love and the life I get to share with them. That is what makes me whole.

FINISH

Lifetime
Member

PLAY
RUGBY
ROUGH, INFORMAL
No experience expected
FRESHMAN, GRAD STUDENTS
and FACULTY ELIGIBLE

Chapter VIII

Stay Out Of The Kitchen

In the early days of retirement, I gave cooking a shot. I decided to make a gourmet soup, thinking, how difficult could this be? Armed with a recipe book and an unjustified sense of confidence, I started tossing ingredients left and right. Unfortunately, my impatience with measuring and my aversion to following directions had a predictably disastrous result. The soup looked fine, but one spoonful told the truth; it was terrible. That experiment did not just ruin dinner, it also made something else clear. Cooking is not my thing, and I had no desire to learn. So, I decided to stay out of the kitchen.

But that did not mean I was off the hook. There are plenty of other ways to contribute around the house, ways that suit my skills and don't result in inedible food. I can vacuum, iron, do yard work, paint, wash floors, and tackle all kinds of other projects. I am also handy at the barbecue grill. As a child, my Mom often asked me to handle the grill while waiting for my Dad to get home from work. Today, my family will tell you that I am the designated expert when it comes to cooking our holiday turkeys on the outdoor grill! The point is simple; I still want to pitch in. I enjoy doing things I'm good at or at least tasks I can complete without breaking something.

All my life, I worked hard to achieve by getting good grades, winning games, earning promotions, and receiving recognition. Those moments did not just mark milestones; they shaped my identity. In retirement, I still crave that sense of accomplishment, but I have realized that it now takes a different form.

Sometimes it's cutting the lawn, finishing a home project, organizing the garage or finally completing that long-delayed paint job. There is no trophy waiting at the end, but there is satisfaction. And every so often, I'll get a well-earned compliment from family or friends. That means the world to me and carries more weight than any plaque ever did.

I have had the experience of driving past a house with a beautifully manicured lawn and thought, I wish my lawn looked like that! Now that I finally have the time, that kind of care and attention feels within reach. But it is not really about the lawn. For me, that well-kept yard is a metaphor. After years of focusing on career, family, deadlines, and responsibilities, retirement gives me the chance to turn toward the things that once sat quietly on the back burner. Maybe that means working on the lawn. Or painting the porch. Or restoring an old piece of furniture. These are not just chores; they are small but meaningful acts of self-care and fulfillment.

Take our hardwood floors, for example. I have a bit of an obsession with them. Our home is nearly a century old and the floors are original. I take real pride in keeping them shiny and well-maintained, which means periodic refinishing and constant vigilance. Sure, it's flattering when someone compliments me on my work but the real reward comes from knowing that I have preserved something with my own hands. Ask my family or close friends, and they will tell you it's not unusual to hear me warn them not to scratch my floors! I say it half in jest but those who know me well also heed the jovial warning

These small accomplishments matter. They represent the shift from doing things because I have to, to doing them because I want to. That is the real gift of retirement. It is the beginning of a new chapter, one where I decide how to spend my time, and what brings meaning to my life.

To live that fully, though, I have learned I have to take care of myself first. A dear friend, Noreen, once shared an airline analogy I never forgot, "put your oxygen mask on first before helping others." If I don't take care of myself physically, mentally, and emotionally, I will not be in a position to care for anyone else.

So I try to keep my house in order in every sense of the word. I focus on what I can do, not what I cannot. And in that balance of projects, relationships, and self-care, I hope to live these years with energy, purpose, and gratitude. If I can do that, perhaps the legacy I leave will be less about what I have built or polished and more about the example of how I lived with intention, with care, and with love.

Chapter IX

Exercise

I work hard to stay physically active. I have discovered that exercise is not just about fitness; it's about freedom, energy, confidence, and the ability to keep doing the things I love. I think of it as preventive maintenance for the years ahead.

There are countless ways to stay active. Many retirees join a fitness club or gym which can provide both structure and social connection. Most gyms have trainers on staff who are more than happy to guide their clients through the basics, set realistic goals, and maintain motivation with personalized routines. When I first retired, I was fortunate that my son, Bryan, took me under his wing. He led me through a two-week boot camp, teaching me core exercises and proper weight-lifting techniques.

One day during a workout, Bryan noticed a man slumped over on a machine. We rushed to help, administered first aid and called 911. By the grace of God, the man survived. In that moment, Bryan and I strengthened not only our commitment to health, but also our bond as father and son.

I now belong to the fitness center at Fairfield University where I enjoy working out in the weight room as well as swimming in the pool. As an alum and retired Director of Rugby, being on campus offers much more than a workout. I love being around the students, many of whom I know through my rugby involvement, and reconnecting with former colleagues. Quite often, I stay to watch a game or match. That vibrant atmosphere leaves me energized long after I head home.

When I want a change of pace from the gym, I head outdoors. Local parks, trails, and the nearby beach provide endless opportunities to walk, jog, stretch, and reset. Nature provides a free and ever-changing gym. Every step outside feels like an investment in both physical and mental health.

Another benefit of outdoor activity is the people I meet along the way. More than once, Mary Lou has wondered why a short walk or jog took so long. I just smile and explain that I went my normal distance but stopped to chat with half the neighborhood.

I will admit that there are days I struggle to motivate myself to get outside. Our solution was simple; we got a dog! Shortly after I retired, Mary Lou and I rescued a puppy we named Bluff, inspired by our coastal surroundings. Bluff requires several walks a day and we are her faithful walking partners. These daily outings add up as we average about five miles a day, in every kind of weather. Neither rain nor snow keeps us inside. The best part is that Mary Lou and I share this time together. Our walks give us space to talk, laugh, or simply enjoy being side by side.

I still make time for the classic activities that I have always loved; golf, skiing, sailing, surfing, fishing, cycling, swimming, and running. These pursuits are more than hobbies; they are joyful ways to stay engaged and challenged. Age does not have to shrink our sense of adventure. If anything, it can expand it. While ziplining or skydiving may not be in my future, another triathlon just might be.

Staying active also means paying attention to diet and medical care. I am the first to admit that diet has always been a challenge for me. My relationship with weight goes back to my high school wrestling days when extreme weight-cutting was routine. I once dropped from 155 pounds to wrestle at 136 by using extreme measures to sweat excessively and barely eat, only to gain much of the weight back within hours after a match. That cycle left a lasting mark.

After my wrestling years, I told myself that I would never diet again. That mindset worked for a while, but not so well as the years passed. Today, I recognize that nutrition plays a vital role in long-term health.

I am equally committed to regular medical care. Like any well-maintained machine, the body requires routine service. My many years in the sun have resulted in semi-annual dermatology visits. Dental appointments, annual physicals, and daily medications are all part of staying ahead of problems rather than reacting to them. Preventative care begins with showing up. Regular checkups today help protect the life I want to enjoy tomorrow.

Retirement is not something that necessarily requires slowing down but it does require a healthy vigilance. By staying active, eating with intention, and committing to preventative care, I give myself the best chance to remain independent, engaged, and fully present. The goal is not to necessarily add years to life but life to the years I have worked so hard to build.

FINISH

Chapter X

Read

The Jesuits got it right. Their timeless motto, Mind, Body, Spirit, reminds us that a well-rounded life needs care in all three areas.

Now let's talk about the mind.

Just like the body, the mind needs regular stimulation to stay strong, sharp, and able to remember where you left your reading glasses. One of the most rewarding ways to exercise the mind is through reading. Books are not just a pleasant way to pass the time, they are fuel for curiosity, creativity, and conversation. Whether I am diving into history, getting lost in fiction, flipping through biographies, or trying to understand philosophers, reading stretches the mind and the imagination.

And the best part? There are more of them than anyone could read in a lifetime. And you don't need to buy a personal library to enjoy them. Public libraries are full of free treasures: print books, audiobooks, e-books, and more. Many even host book clubs or discussion groups, a wonderful opportunity for those of us who enjoy talking about books almost as much as reading them.

When I was in college, I took Evelyn Wood's speed-reading course, also known as Reading Dynamics. It is a system for dramatically increasing reading speed and comprehension by eliminating subvocalization (sounding out words) and using a finger or pointer to guide the eyes across groups of words, focusing on overall meaning rather than individual words. It is a technique that became popular in the 1950's and trained millions, including U.S. presidents, to process information faster. The method is designed to unlock natural reading potential making for faster and more efficient reading. It is an amazing tool and incredibly useful for absorbing a massive amount of information. My roommate, Rich, used to threaten to tie my hands behind my back so that I would become illiterate!

Back when I had a 120-mile weekly commute, I became well acquainted with books on tape. Over nineteen years, I listened to hundreds of titles including War and Peace. These days, I enjoy reading at my own pace, ideally in a beach chair with my feet in the sand and no traffic in sight.

Reading comes in many shapes and sizes and hardly a day goes by when I am not reading in one form or another. I find it especially peaceful to spend a few quiet minutes each day picking up the Bible and reading a few verses. At the other end of the spectrum, it is nearly impossible these days to avoid reading something on social media or searching Google for information. One of my greatest pleasures is reading a bedtime story to my grandchildren, bringing back fond memories of the nights I read to my own children. And, once a year, I am treated to a cherished tradition by reading 'Twas The Night Before Christmas!

Of course, reading is not the only way to keep the mind humming. Films, TV shows, and sports all offer different kinds of mental stimulation. A great movie or series can take me around the world, introduce me to different cultures, and stir up my emotions sometimes all in one sitting and without leaving my living room. Documentaries can be enlightening, and a well-done comedy can make me laugh out loud which I consider to be a legitimate form of therapy.

Sports are another favorite. Whether it is football, baseball, basketball, hockey, or golf, there is always something to follow. It is a mental workout to keep up with stats, strategy, and names that I can't quite pronounce but it's fun trying. Sometimes I even find myself yelling at the TV as if it can hear me. Sports also offer connection: the joy of celebrating wins, the camaraderie of shared losses, and the age-old ritual of shouting advice to professional athletes who somehow don't take it.

The key is balance. Too much passive screen time and the brain might start resembling a remote control. That's why I like to mix it up. Read a great book one day, watch a big game the next, and maybe stream a good film another day. And of course, it's always fun to chat about it over coffee with a friend. That is what keeps the mind sharp and the spirit smiling.

Retirement gives me a gift that I have craved for decades; it gives me time. And with that time comes the opportunity not just to relax but also to grow. With books, films, sports, and good company, I can keep my mind active and my conversations interesting for many vibrant years to come.

JAMES PATTERSON
John Grisham
THE JUDGE'S LIST

Chapter XI

Share Your Joy

I grew up on a dead-end street named Ashwood Drive. My Mom often told me that, as a little boy, I would wander the neighborhood carrying a hammer. I never hit anyone with it; I just carried it around. To this day, I still feel an odd attraction to hammers, even though everyone who knows me is well aware that I have no idea of how to properly use one.

At the end of the street there was a thick wooded area. My brother, Kevin, along with his friends built a fort for my friend Rodd and me. It was only one of many forts constructed in those woods. In fact, there were so many that we named the area Fort Ashwood. We spent countless hours there and, to this day, some of my finest memories come from that place.

I mention Fort Ashwood because it brought me great joy, so much so that even the memory of it still has that effect on me. Looking back, I think three things contributed to that joy.

The first was accomplishment. Together, with the help of my brother and others, we had something for which we were responsible and could proudly call our own.

Second was community. Our fort was one of several and, at a very young age, I experienced the true meaning of neighborhood. We shared common ground, worked together, and supported one another in achieving similar goals.

Third was respect. We respected each other's space and values. We were friends and we treated one another with kindness and compassion. It was a simple but powerful example of what it means to love your neighbor.

Fort Ashwood brought me joy. Little did I know it at the time, but that kind of joy would become something I would seek, recognize, and cherish throughout my life.

I know that my son had similar experiences in his youth while building forts with his friends, and my daughters share the same values. Now I see those values being passed down to my grandchildren. They don't know it, but I recently checked out their newly constructed fort. It brings a huge smile to my face! May their "Fort Ashwood" be a catalyst for their joy as well.

Everyone knows that it is nearly impossible to replicate an especially memorable experience. However, many years later, Mary Lou and I rediscovered Fort Ashwood when we moved to our little hamlet of Lordship. For us, our neighborhood embodies those same three qualities of accomplishment, community, and respect which bring us great joy.

A clear sign of fellowship is evident while walking along the sidewalks, on the beach, or past a neighbor's yard. It is not unusual to be acknowledged with a genuine greeting. Even when someone doesn't know your name, there is sincere interest in your well-being through a smile, a wave, or a brief conversation that feels real. It's the kind of place where you feel seen, welcomed, and connected, and where kindness is not an exception but the norm.

Lordship is home to a Father's Club that captures the very essence of what it means to belong. Founded in 1947, the Lordship Father's Club (LFC) works alongside the Lordship Improvement Association (LIA), which dates back to 1924. While the LIA's important mission is to enhance and preserve the distinct character and natural beauty of the Lordship waterfront for all residents, the LFC focuses on organizing family-friendly events for all ages.

Each year the club hosts activities such as an Easter egg hunt, Mother's Tea, Halloween parade, Bands on the Bluffs, fishing derby, Lordship Olympics, spelling bee, and Breakfast with Santa. These events encourage participation, connection, and volunteerism while preserving traditions and building lasting memories for local families.

We have been members of both the LIA and LFC since arriving in Lordship nearly a half century ago. I am deeply honored to have been awarded lifetime membership in the Lordship Father's Club in recognition of my longtime service, one of the greatest honors of my life.

In my second grade Sunday school class, I tell my students on the first day of class that I give homework. After listening to the sighing and groaning, I chuckle and tell the kids that the homework assignment is to do something nice for someone at least once a week. I don't care what they do even if it is just a simple smile.

I ask them, "did you ever receive a smile from someone?" Of course they have. That smile can bring brightness to anyone's day! It is very difficult to receive a smile from someone and not to smile back. Try it!

The kicker is that I tell my students that this homework assignment is for the next 97 years. So, if you happen to live to be more than 104 years old, you're off the hook from continuing to do my homework assignment! As I often remind my students, no matter how busy life gets, there is always time to give someone a smile.

Now, with fewer demands on my schedule, I am aware that I have even more opportunities to brighten someone's day. Maybe it is visiting someone who is sick or lonely, making a quick call to an old friend, holding the door for a stranger, volunteering at church, returning a neighbor's garbage can, or simply picking up litter on my morning walk. These small gestures require very little effort, but they make a big difference.

Just recently, I had a wonderful reminder. I was working in the yard when I received a text from my daughter; the school was looking for volunteers to sit in the dunk tank at my grandsons' sixth-grade picnic. Without hesitation, I dropped everything and headed to the school. A short while later, I was soaked, surrounded by laughter, and witnessing the sheer joy on the faces of my grandsons and their classmates. It was a priceless moment and a memory that I will always cherish and I'm pretty sure that they will as well.

There is a lesson in all of this: be open to unexpected opportunities, be flexible enough to change plans, and always remember the importance of family.

The beauty of doing these kinds of selfless acts is found when no one notices. The intention is not doing them for praise or recognition; it is simply because it's the right thing to do. Sometimes, the best acts of kindness are the quiet ones, shared only between an individual and the Good Lord above.

MAY 2025

Spelling Bee

Lordship School APR

Chapter XII

Travel….Focused & Meaningful

One of the first questions people tend to ask when someone retires is, "are you going to travel?" It's a logical question. The assumption, of course, is that during our working years, especially while raising a family, there is rarely enough time to explore the world.

Even staying within the U.S. offers more adventures than one could possibly check off in one lifetime. Throw in Europe, Asia, South America, and beyond, and it starts to feel like a full-time job just choosing where to go.

Having spent a good portion of my career on the road, I don't feel a burning need to become a globetrotter in retirement. So, Mary Lou and I pick our spots carefully. As with most things in life, moderation is key. We think about the kinds of places we would truly enjoy, the people we would love to meet, and the experiences we hope to have. We also factor in our energy level, our schedule, and, yes, our budget. We make a plan that works for us.

So instead of racking up airline miles, we have chosen to keep our travel aspirations focused and meaningful. We love short getaways: a few days skiing with my brothers in Utah, a weekend away with friends, our annual family vacation to the Jersey Shore or a relaxing stay at our favorite bed & breakfast in Newport.

For our 50th wedding anniversary, we decided to go big. We traveled to Dublin to watch Ireland play France at Aviva Stadium during the Six Nations rugby tournament. We stayed at the Shelbourne Hotel which also happened to be hosting the Irish national team. Mary Lou was in her glory, chatting up the players and collecting photo ops like autographs at a rock concert!

After Dublin, we spent a night with close friends Noreen and Denis in Cork. During our visit, Denis took us to Blarney Castle. Mary Lou, not a fan of heights, stayed safely on the ground while I climbed to the top to kiss the Blarney Stone. It had been nearly 50 years since my last smooch with the stone, and I figured I could use a refresher to enhance my gift of gab!

Then it was off to Paris! It was Mary Lou's first time in the City of Light which made it especially meaningful for her as an artist. After being duped only once by a street hustler and mistakenly trying to wing it without a planned itinerary, we quickly learned that in Paris, reservations are not just helpful, they are essential. Once we got that sorted, we explored Notre Dame, the Louvre, Musée d'Orsay, the Eiffel Tower and a long list of breathtaking sights. A magical dinner cruise along the Seine aboard the Bateaux Mouche was a fitting end to what we now refer to as our trip of a lifetime.

As I mentioned earlier, we are truly blessed to live in a beautiful beach community surrounded by friends and family. A big part of our joy comes not from flying across the world but from staying close to home. We love spending time at the beach: sailing, sunbathing, fishing, taking long walks, and simply enjoying the kind of camaraderie that retirement makes possible.

The bottom line? I am finding that, in retirement, travel does not have to mean nonstop motion or a passport full of stamps. It is not about how far we go, it's about what brings us joy. Sometimes that joy is Paris in the spring. At other times, it's just a quiet afternoon on the sand with the people we love.

I do still have one lingering bucket list item: skiing the Alps. Hey, a guy can dream!

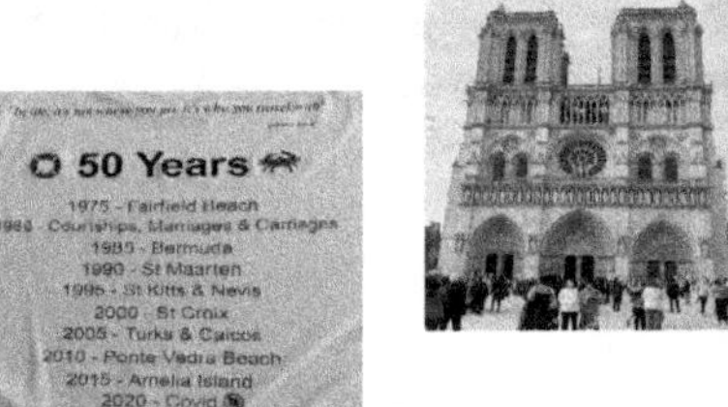
50 Years
1975 - Fairfield Beach
Courtships, Marriages & Carriages
1985 - Bermuda
1990 - St Maarten
1995 - St Kitts & Nevis
2000 - St Croix
2005 - Turks & Caicos
2010 - Ponte Vedra Beach
2015 - Amelia Island
2020 - Covid
2025 - Key West
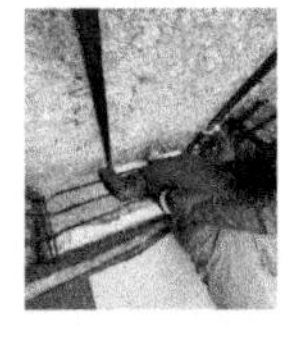

Chapter XIII

Believe in Santa Claus

One of the many wonderful gifts that God has provided each of us is a vivid imagination. I have believed in Santa Claus for as long as I can remember and that belief has had a lasting impact on my life, especially now in retirement. I have found that childhood memories seem to come alive more vividly during this stage of life. As children, excitement and imagination are fresh and new. As adults in our golden years, we are given the opportunity to revisit some of our most imaginative and thrilling experiences both for ourselves and, perhaps even more meaningfully, through our loved ones.

According to the Encyclopedia Britannica, Santa Claus is a legendary figure who is the traditional patron of Christmas in the United States and other countries, bringing gifts to children. His popular image is rooted in traditions associated with Saint Nicholas, a fourth-century Christian saint often depicted in red bishop's robes.

Santa Claus is said to live at the North Pole with his wife, Mrs. Claus, where he spends the year making toys with the help of his elves. There, he receives letters from children asking for Christmas gifts. On Christmas Eve, he loads his sleigh with toys and flies around the world pulled by eight or sometimes nine reindeer, stopping at each child's home. He slides down the chimney, leaves gifts, and refreshes himself with the milk and cookies thoughtfully left by the household's children.

For those who may be non-believers, I refer you to the famous editorial "Yes, Virginia, there is a Santa Claus." Written in 1897 by Francis Pharcellus Church for the New York Sun, the article responded to young Virginia O'Hanlon's question about Santa's existence. Church eloquently addressed skepticism by emphasizing the enduring importance of faith, imagination, and the magic of childhood along with the deeper spirit of Christmas.

I have had the great fortune of playing the role of Santa Claus for the past forty-five years! It began when neighbors who owned an appliance store asked if I would portray Santa during the Christmas season. Each year they rented me a Santa suit, and I happily stepped into the role of the jolly old elf bringing joy to countless children. One of the most special moments for me was having my own children sit on my lap, gazing at me with eyes that saw Santa Claus, not their dad.

When I put on that Santa suit, something almost miraculous happens; I become Santa Claus. One year after leaving the appliance store, I was heading to a party where Santa was scheduled to greet guests and their children. While driving on the Merrit Parkway, I noticed a broken-down car and its driver who was hitchhiking for help. Imagine his surprise when Santa pulled over to rescue him! Naturally, I drove him several towns away to his home. This was long before cell phones so I had no way to let my wife, Mary Lou, know that I would be late. When I finally arrived at the party, she asked where I had been. I simply told her that once you put on that suit, you truly become Santa Claus and there was no way I could leave a traveler stranded on the highway!

In 1989, several friends and I suggested to our local Father's Club that they sponsor a "Breakfast with Santa." More than thirty-five years later, along with a host of volunteers, yours truly continues to bring cheer and merriment to the local children and their families during the Christmas season. Today, reminiscent of my own children over forty years ago, I have the joy of having my grandchildren sit on my lap while looking at me with believing eyes, seeing Santa Claus and not their grandfather. The look of a child gazing into the eyes of Santa is uniquely indescribable!

Santa can bring Christmas joy directly into the homes of family and neighbors. Imagine the excitement of Santa Claus knocking on your front door for a personal visit and a photo by your Christmas tree! I witness the wonderment of Christmas not only through the eyes of children but also though their parents who so deeply want to hold on to their own childhood memories.

As the family patriarch, I have been given the privilege to read 'Twas the Night Before Christmas to all my grandchildren after Christmas Eve dinner. Words cannot adequately describe the delight that I have with this experience. It is truly one of the highlights of my life!

For years, I have been collecting letters and Christmas lists written by my children and now my grandchildren. I keep them in a special place and plan to share these treasures with each of them at some future date. That alone brings me great personal joy; but I also return the favor by writing each child an individually crafted letter by Santa himself. I am hopeful that, in some small way, these personalized notes keep their childlike imaginations ignited so that one day they, too, will pass that sense of wonder on to future generations.

Even our annual Christmas card reflects this tradition, usually featuring Santa engaged in some beachside activity. Over the years Santa has been sailing, surfing, and even water skiing. The question each year is always the same; what will Santa be doing this year?

For me, perhaps now more than ever in retirement, the privilege of playing Santa Claus has been a significant and deeply meaningful part of my life. It keeps me connected to the imaginations of my youth and, more importantly, allows me to pass along joy, wonder, and nostalgic innocence to children and adults alike.

Yes, Virginia, There is a Santa Claus

Dear Editor—
I am 8 years old. Some of my little friends say there is no Santa Claus. Papa says, "If you see it in The Sun, it's so." Please tell me the truth, is there a Santa Claus?
Virginia O'Hanlon

Chapter XIV

The Value of Experience

Retirement is often described as the end of something; yet it rarely feels that way from the inside. What ends is the routine, the calendar, the deadlines and the expectations that once shaped each day. What remains is something far less visible but far more durable, the experience gathered over a lifetime.

Something that really invigorates me is when a young person asks for my advice or help. I cannot describe the elation that I felt when a dear family friend once reached out for advice. He received my guidance with gratitude and gave it serious consideration as he made his decision.

Moments like that remind me of just how blessed I am to have close relationships with each of my family members and to be trusted when they turn to me for advice. That kind of trust is never accidental nor is it something I take lightly. It is built over years of shared experiences, honest conversations, and learning when to listen more than to speak. I am reminded of a scene from my favorite movie, It's a Wonderful Life, when a young George Bailey, unsure of himself, sees a simple sign in Mr. Gower's drugstore: "Ask Dad, he knows."

In my role as an advisor to the Fairfield University Rugby Club, many student-athletes have sought my help with networking as they pursue employment after graduation. The satisfaction that comes from helping someone successfully find a job is indescribable!

I believe that young people too often neglect to seek the advice of retirees. Regretfully, even in my own life, I did not often seek the advice of seasoned veterans. My Dad frequently tried to offer advice, but I was often too stubborn to listen. In retrospect, I know that he was usually right; to this day I regret not paying closer attention. I suppose I mistakenly believed that he was biased or did not fully understand my situation. I now realize how wrong I was and feel the sting of that realization.

One day, during the time we owned our restaurant, I found a note from my father on my desk. It said, "It's going to work!" It was signed, "Dad." At the time, I probably thought that he was referring to the success of the restaurant. However, knowing my Dad, I think he was looking at the big picture. In the those few words, I think he was telling me the same thing that he told me as a young man. He was encouraging me to keep my head down and work hard. He was right! Although the restaurant was not as successful as we had hoped, it all came together and life turned out just fine. To this day, I keep that framed note on my desk and reflect upon it just about every day. Thanks, Dad!

It is inevitable that we will all grow older and enter the so-called senior years. While we experience the occasional "senior moment," it does not mean that we no longer provide value to others. Our experiences and life lessons are invaluable, and it is important that we share them.

We need to embrace these twilight years and enjoy the freedom and romance that they bring. Our neighborhoods and communities offer countless opportunities to come together, meet new people, share experiences, and provide insight, expertise, and perspective to younger generations.

Sometimes the word retirement becomes synonymous with getting older. As a result, many of us begin to feel uncomfortable even within familiar surroundings including amongst our own family members.

I recently came across an anonymous reflection online about caring for aging parents. It is one of those ideas that tends to resurface in quiet moments when life slows down just enough to think clearly. It speaks less about aging itself and more about how we choose to show up for those who once showed up for us.

At its core, it is a reminder that this stage of life is not about being managed or set aside, but about being seen, heard, and respected. It calls for the younger generation to offer the same patience, dignity, and grace that was once so freely given to them, often without their even realizing it at the time.

Perhaps that is the real continuity between generations: not authority or dependence, but mutual respect carried forward in different forms. The roles may change, but the value of presence, attention, and love does not.

This perspective also reshapes how we think about our own later years. Rather than a withdrawal from life, it can be a deepening of it. There is more space now to listen, to observe, to encourage, and to share what has been learned along the way without the urgency that once defined earlier stages of life.

In many ways, retirement offers a different kind of contribution, one not driven by titles or deadlines, but by availability. Being present when someone needs direction, reassurance, or simply a listening ear. These moments may seem small, but they often carry more weight than we realize.

There is also something to be said for the freedom that comes with this stage. The freedom to choose where to invest time, which relationships to nurture, and how to stay connected to the world around us. Communities, families, and organizations all benefit when experience is not withdrawn, but shared.

The challenge is not simply to grow older, but to remain engaged and to continue to offer insight, encouragement, and perspective wherever it is welcomed. In doing so, we not only stay connected to others, but also remain connected to a sense of purpose that does not diminish with age.

In the end, retirement is not so much a line we cross but more like a new way of living the same life. The pace may change and the responsibilities may shift, but the opportunity to matter to others and to ourselves remains.

What becomes important is not what I no longer do, but what I still have to offer: experience, patience, perspective, and the ability to listen. These are not diminished by age; they are refined by it.

There is quiet satisfaction in realizing that I am still needed and still able to contribute in ways that may not always be visible. That may happen in a conversation that helps someone find direction, a moment of encouragement, or a word spoken at just the right time.

Perhaps just as important, there is wisdom in receiving as well as giving by allowing younger generations to bring their energy, ideas, and questions into my life, just as I once brought mine into theirs.

This stage of life can be one of the most meaningful not only because it slows down but also because it becomes clearer about what matters, about where we are most useful, and about the importance of simply being present for one another.

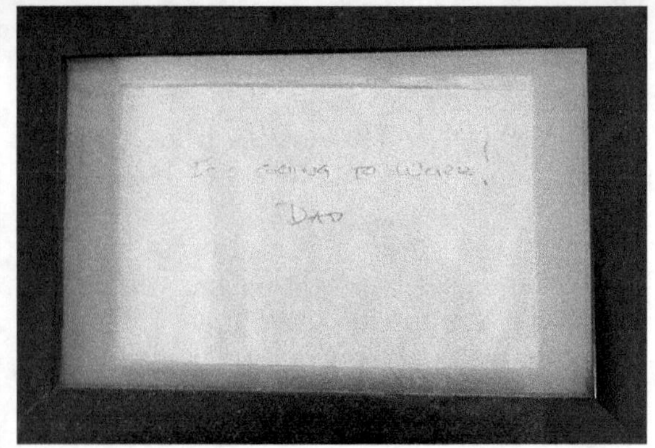
Dad

Ask Dad,
he knows
SWEET CAPORAL

Chapter XV

Have Fun

Who doesn't want to have fun? But having fun is not always as simple as it sounds. Life does not stop being complicated just because we have stepped into retirement. Our minds may still be preoccupied with financial concerns, health issues, family matters, or simply the lingering habit of always being busy. And many of us forget that fun requires effort. It doesn't just happen; we must seek it, make room for it, and give ourselves permission to enjoy it.

That idea may feel difficult at first, but it should not be discouraging. We have spent years working, raising families, and meeting obligations. For most of our lives, fun was a secondary priority, something squeezed into weekends or vacations if time allowed. Now the script has flipped. This phase of life is about reclaiming joy and that might take a little practice.

I started by talking to people I trust, those who genuinely care about my well-being. My wife, children, grandchildren, and close friends were all helpful. I made a mental list of things I enjoy. I did not pressure myself to figure it all out at once. I simply began trying things to see what resonated.

I also tried to keep it fresh and varied so I would not fall into a rut. My interests tend to shift with the seasons. In summer, I might take an early morning bike ride or swim in the pool. In winter, I may head to the mountains for a day of skiing or just cozy up by the fireplace with a good book. Fun is personal. What delights one person might bore another and that is totally fine.

Just recently, I tagged along with two of my daughters, Kate and Colleen, and their children for a day of skiing. As a passionate, lifelong skier, I can hardly describe the elation I felt sharing the slopes with my children and grandchildren, three generations participating together in an activity we equally enjoy, each bringing our own experience to the day. We were not only building memories, but we were also fully present in the moment together. And the coolest part of all? I could still keep up with them!

That day on the mountain was not an isolated moment. It reminded me of how often my greatest connections with my children have come through shared experiences, especially the ones that involve a little movement, a little challenge and a lot of laughter. There was a time my daughter, Erin, invited me to participate in a Warrior Dash with her. Who but she, broken finger and all, would think that an event built around obstacles, athletic skill and copious amounts of mud would make for an ideal father-daughter bonding experience? Somehow, it was just that. We had a blast, got thoroughly filthy and lived to tell about it!

My son, Bryan, and I tend to bond in a slightly more civilized setting, the golf course. He usually invites me to be his partner in a local golf tournament as a Father's Day gift. While golf may sound far less extreme than skiing down a mountain or crawling through mud, we still manage to turn it into an adventure. Between our usual father-son antics in the golf cart and the occasional practical joke on the other twosome, we laugh until our bellies ache. We always walk away with a memorable experience, even if the final golf score somehow slips our minds.

Looking back, I realize that these moments matter not only because of the activity itself but also because of the time that we spend together. Whether on snowy slopes, muddy trails, or manicured fairways, the real joy has always been in sharing the experience and being fully present, totally engaged and grateful for every chance to keep up.

I have also learned not to be afraid of being a beginner again. Retirement gives me the freedom to explore new interests without the pressure to perform. I don't need to be good at something to enjoy it; I just need to be open.

For example, although I had dabbled in golf for many years, I was never very good and, frankly, did not enjoy it. After I retired, my son suggested that I join a Monday morning golf league at a local course. I had no interest but, at his urging, I agreed to give it a try. I'm still not very good at golf but for the first time in my life, I actually look forward to Mondays. I enjoy the game and the camaraderie of league play so much that I joined a second league on Tuesdays at another course! My enthusiasm was so contagious that my wife even joined a women's league.

I have come to believe that spontaneity matters. Some of my most enjoyable experiences have grown out of a sudden change in plans or an unexpected opportunity. One of the great gifts of retirement is a calendar that is not always full, or at least one that is flexible enough to allow for the occasional impulse.

From time to time, a group of old ruggers meet in New York City for dinner and drinks to catch up and reminisce. The stories are usually the same as the last time we got together, though still funny and, on occasion, slightly embellished.

At our most recent gathering, four of us made an impulsive decision to play golf in the Bronx on our way down from Connecticut. Instead of taking a late-afternoon train, we drove to Pelham and squeezed in a round before heading into the city to meet the rest of the group. After a beautiful day on the links, we continued with an evening filled with laughter and good company amongst our rugby mates. These reunions are always enjoyable, but this little twist made the day especially memorable, though I wouldn't mind forgetting my golf score.

During the COVID days, the NY Times introduced a game called WORDLE.

About a dozen of my college friends and I saw an opportunity to use it to stay connected in addition to our bi-weekly cocktail Zoom meetings. Rather than invent something new, we adapted a familiar framework, a golf scorecard. A score of four is par, three is a birdie, and so on. The highest WORDLE score is seven so that became our maximum. The scorecard looks just like a golf card with eighteen "holes." Each player antes up five dollars per game toward the prize pool. As commissioner, I track scores daily on a spreadsheet. At the end of eighteen holes, cash prizes go to the top three finishers along with a small stipend for the "caboose," or last place finisher. As we have just completed our 78th round as of this writing (1,422 consecutive games over nearly four years), we have even established handicaps to keep things competitive. We now have four annual "majors": The Gonzaga, The Loyola, The Campion, and The Regis, named after our Jesuit dormitories at our alma mater, Fairfield University. WORDLE satisfies our competitive instincts while giving us a daily connection, one that has kept friendships of over fifty years vibrant and alive.

Having fun can take many forms. Once a month, our local chapter of the Knights of Columbus meets to collect food for those in need. Several of us gather on a Saturday morning to volunteer for this worthwhile cause. While we are doing something good by donating our time to help others, we are also having fun. Working together in service, sharing a few laughs, and enjoying one another's company turns effort into fellowship. It is an experience that we all look forward to each month.

Most importantly, I have come to understand that fun is a gateway to joy and a deeper, more sustaining emotion. Joy is not fleeting or surface-level. It is a deep contentment that comes from knowing that I am living fully and meaningfully. It is found in laughter, in connection, in discovery, and in quiet moments of peace. It is about being present.

It feels fitting that this is the final chapter. Throughout this book, I have explored the importance of nurturing my spirit, caring for my body, engaging my mind, and staying active and connected. Together, these have helped lay a strong foundation for joy.

I have found it important to give myself permission to smile more. Laugh more. Try more. Stumble and get back up. Be silly. Be spontaneous. Have fun. After all, I've earned it.

Retirement is not the end of the road. It is the beginning of a new, uncharted chapter and one filled with opportunity, reflection, and purpose. I see this time as a chance to rediscover who I am without the deadlines, the demands, or the distractions.

Whether I am strengthening my faith, enjoying a quiet walk while holding hands with my wife, tending the garden, learning something new, laughing with old friends, or simply sitting in stillness, I try to find joy in both the extraordinary and the everyday. Sometimes that joy comes in the smallest of ways like finding a piece of sea glass on the beach, holding a grandchild close, or sharing a moment of prayer that grounds me in gratitude. I embrace this chapter of life with curiosity and courage. And most of all, I try to remember that the best is not behind me but still ahead.

Retirement is my island in the sun. And it is my sincere intention to make it count!

SAUTE
SLUMP
SKULL
KATE KEARNEY'S

Acknowledgments

This book would not have come to life without the encouragement, guidance, and support of many people who mean a great deal to me.

First and foremost, I owe a special debt of gratitude to my dear friend, Christine Anderson, an accomplished author whose insight, patience, and generosity helped shape this work from its early stages. She spent countless hours reviewing drafts, offering thoughtful edits, and encouraging me to see this project in a broader and more personal light. Her steady support and honest feedback were invaluable throughout the journey and I am deeply grateful for her friendship, as well as that of her husband, Rodd.

I would also like to thank Dan Mariani, who offered encouragement and helpful perspective during the later stages of this manuscript. His willingness to step in, share advice, and lend his support at a critical time is sincerely appreciated.

My heartfelt thanks go to my family and close friends who provided encouragement, patience, and thoughtful feedback along the way. Their belief in me made this process far more meaningful than I ever expected. Many thanks to my daughter, Colleen, for providing final editing and layout support prior to publication.

Above all, I give thanks to God for His many blessings, for the opportunities I have been given, and for the guidance to continue striving to make the most of the gifts entrusted to me.

www.ingramcontent.com/pod-product-compliance
Lightning Source LLC
LaVergne TN
LVHW010629100826
845148LV00014B/3167

* 9 7 9 8 2 3 4 0 5 9 0 8 6 *